Columbia University

Statutes Enacted by the Trustees of Columbia College

Vol. 2

Columbia University

Statutes Enacted by the Trustees of Columbia College
Vol. 2

ISBN/EAN: 9783337370978

Printed in Europe, USA, Canada, Australia, Japan

Cover: Foto ©Suzi / pixelio.de

More available books at **www.hansebooks.com**

Columbia College

STATUTES ENACTED

BY THE

TRUSTEES OF COLUMBIA COLLEGE

IN THE CITY OF NEW YORK

NEW YORK
PRINTED FOR THE COLLEGE
MAY, 1890

CONTENTS.

TRUSTEES OF COLUMBIA COLLEGE.

v

STATUTES.

PART I.

GENERAL PROVISIONS.

CHAPTER I.

OF THE PRESIDENT.

§ 1. The President of the College shall be the president of every faculty established by the trustees. He shall, when present, preside at all commencements, and shall sign all diplomas for degrees duly conferred.

He shall, when present, preside at all meetings of the several faculties, and his concurrence shall be necessary to every act of each of the faculties; unless, after his non-concurrence, the act or resolution shall be again passed by the vote of two-thirds of the entire faculty at the same or at the next succeeding meeting of the faculty.

In case the faculty be equally divided, the president shall have a casting vote, in addition to his vote as a member of the faculty.

In all cases where there shall be a non-concurrence between the president and a majority of the faculty present at the time, the names of those voting on each side shall be entered on the minutes of the faculty, and each member of the faculty shall be entitled to have entered on the minutes his reasons, presented at the time (in writing), for his vote.

§ 2. It shall be the duty of the president to take charge and have care of the college generally, of its buildings, of the grounds adjacent thereto, and of its movable property upon the same;

To see that the course of instruction and discipline is faithfully pursued;

To call meetings of the several faculties, and to give such directions and perform such acts as shall, in his judgment, promote the interests of the college, so that they do not contravene the charter, the statutes, the orders of the trustees, or the decisions of the several faculties;

To visit the class-rooms from time to time, and keep himself informed of the manner in which the classes are taught;

To report to the trustees annually, at the stated meeting in October, and as occasion shall require, the state of the college, and particularly the manner in which the several professors and tutors, and other officers, perform their respective duties.

§ 3. In the absence or disability of the president, the senior professor in the School of Arts, who shall be in the regular performance of his duties, shall perform the duties and exercise the authority of the president.

CHAPTER II.

OF THE FACULTIES.

§ 1. The several faculties shall have power in their respective schools from time to time (subject to the reserved power of control by the trustees):

To fix the requirements of admission, the course of study and the conditions of graduation;

To establish rules for ascertaining the proficiency of students, and for determining their relative standing;

To establish the rules of conduct to be observed by the students, and to punish infractions of the same;

To adjudge rewards and punishments;

To make all such regulations of their own proceedings, and for the better government of their respective schools, as shall not contravene the charter of the college, the statutes, or any order of the trustees.

§ 2. No exercise of the powers conferred on any of the faculties which may change the terms of admission to any school, or the course of instruction in the same, or the requirements of graduation, shall take effect until at least ninety days after the same shall have been submitted to the trustees.

§ 3. Appointments of all officers of grades inferior to

that of adjunct or assistant professor, including fellows, prize lecturers, and tutors, shall be made by the faculties severally of the schools in which such officers are to serve, subject to confirmation by the trustees; the number and the grade of all such officers and the amount of their compensation being determined by the trustees.

§ 4. Each faculty shall keep a book of minutes of its proceedings, which shall be submitted by the president to the trustees at their meetings.

§ 5. No officer engaged in instruction shall be employed in any occupation which interferes with the thorough, efficient, and earnest performance of the duties of his office.

§ 6. The professors in the several schools shall take precedence according to the dates of their appointments.

§ 7. It shall be the duty of the professors, instructors, and tutors, to assist the president with their counsel and co-operation.

§ 8. The professors, instructors, and other officers, in the several schools, shall present themselves and be ready for duty at the college in the week preceding the first Monday in October, and shall continue in attendance until the close of the exercises on commencement day, except on holidays, or when granted leave of absence by the trustees, or as temporarily excused by the president.

CHAPTER III.

OF THE LIBRARY.

§ 1. The president shall, subject to the trustees and the committee on the library, have the general charge and control of the library and the rooms containing it, and also of the expenditures of all moneys appropriated by the trustees for the purchase of books and supplies therefor; he shall appoint all needed assistants and subordinate officers, and fix their titles, duties, and compensations, provided that the total amount shall not exceed the appropriation of the trustees for that purpose; he shall regularly report all such appointments to the trustees; he shall make and enforce by suitable penalties any needed rules and regulations relating to the library, its readers, officers, or servants; and, unless otherwise specially ordered by the trustees, he shall have charge of all matters pertaining to the college library, and the custody of all college publications, works of art and historical interest, etc., belonging to the college, and shall make annual examinations of the same, and fix their place of deposit, and may make any needed regulations to increase their usefulness or secure their safety.

§ 2. The librarian shall be the executive officer of the library, under the direction of the president, and shall attend to the execution of all orders, votes, directions, and regulations. He shall be the custodian of the property of the library, and of its files, records, books and papers, and shall, when required by the committee on the library, keep full record of their proceedings, send notices, conduct correspondence, and sign and issue orders. All bills on account of the library, for books, periodicals, binding supplies, administration, or other expenses, shall be examined and certified by the librarian, or, in his absence, by the deputy duly appointed, and countersigned by the president, before being paid.

CHAPTER IV.

OF OTHER OFFICERS OF THE COLLEGE.

§ 1. It shall be the duty of the superintendent, under the direction of the president, to take charge of the boiler house and of the heating, ventilating, and lighting apparatus; to employ, control, and discharge all persons employed in and about the said boiler house and apparatus, and all janitors, watchmen, and other subordinates and servants; to keep the entire grounds of the college and all the buildings thereon, and the sidewalks surrounding the grounds, clean and free from dust, dirt, snow, and ice, and to care for the coat rooms of the college and of its schools; and he shall have care of the college grounds and buildings and of the furniture and fixtures therein, and shall see that the same are kept in good and proper order and in sufficient repair, and shall perform such other duties as may from time to time be imposed upon him by the president, or the committee on buildings and grounds, or the trustees.

§ 2. It shall be the duty of the proctor, under the direction of the president, to preserve and maintain peace and order within the college precincts, and to report all violations thereof to the president. He shall also, so far as proper attention to his regular duties will permit, discharge such duties in the library as may be assigned to him by the president.

CHAPTER V.

OF STUDENTS.

§ 1. Every student will be required, as a condition of admission to any school, and subsequently at the beginning of each succeeding academic year, to write in the matriculation book to be kept in the president's office, his own name and the name, place of abode, and post-office address of his father or guardian ; and this book shall indicate the school or schools in which the student is conducting his studies. The matriculation fee shall be five dollars.

§ 2. None but matriculated students or graduates of the college shall be allowed to attend any of the classes without the special permission of the trustees.

§ 3. Tuition fees shall be paid on matriculation, provided, however, that all tuition fees exceeding one hundred dollars ($100) per annum will be paid semi-annually, one half at the commencement of each session of the college year.

§ 4. An honorable discharge shall always be granted to any student in good standing, who may desire to withdraw from the college ; but no undergraduate of the School of Arts or the School of Mines, under the age of twenty-one years, shall be entitled to a discharge without the assent of his parent or guardian, given in writing to the president.

§ 5. So soon as a student shall have been admitted to any school, he shall be presented with a copy of these statutes, and of any printed rules and by-laws made under them for the government of the students by the faculty of the school.

§ 6. Any matriculated student, except students in the undergraduate classes of the School of Arts and the School of Mines, may attend any combination of courses permitted by the president, by and with the advice of the university council. Such student shall pay the fee proper to the school in which he takes the greatest number of hours.

CHAPTER VI.

OF FREE SCHOLARSHIPS.

§ 1. The Alumni Association of Columbia College shall be entitled to have always, in the undergraduate department of the School of Arts, four students to be instructed free of charge.

§ 2. The Society for Promoting Religion and Learning in the State of New York shall be entitled to have always, in the undergraduate department of the School of Arts, two students in each class, to be instructed free of charge.

§ 3. The members of the Board of the College, the professors of the School of Mines, of the Law School, and of the School of Political Science, and the chaplain of the college, shall be entitled to have their sons educated in any school of the college free of charge.

§ 4. The above privileges are subject to the regulations of the trustees in regard to the standing and scholarship of persons allowed free tuition.

CHAPTER VII.

OF FOUNDATIONS.

§ 1. Any person or persons who may found a scholarship, by the payment of not less than two thousand dollars to the treasurer of the college, shall be entitled to have always one student educated in the college free of all charges for tuition. This right may be transferred to others. The scholarship shall bear such name as the founder or founders may designate.

§ 2. Any person or persons who shall endow a professorship in the classics, in political, mathematical, or physical science, or in the literature of any of the ancient or modern languages, by the payment of not less than one hundred thousand dollars to the treasurer of the college, shall forever have the right of nominating a professor for the same, subject to the approbation of the trustees, who shall hold his office by the same tenure as the other professors of the college—the nomination to be made by the person or persons who shall make the endowment, or such person or persons as he or they may designate. The proceeds of the endowment shall be appropriated to the salary of the professor.

CHAPTER VIII.

OF COMMENCEMENTS.

§ 1. There shall be an annual commencement on the second Wednesday in June, when degrees shall be conferred in all the schools.

At the commencement there shall be exhibited such literary or other performances as the several faculties, with the approval of the trustees, may direct.

§ 2. Should there, among the exercises so ordered, be any orations or addresses from members of the graduating classes, all such performances shall be previously submitted for criticism to the president, and no student who shall refuse or neglect to adopt the corrections or amendments pointed out to him, or who shall deliver his oration or exercise otherwise than is approved by the president, shall receive his degree.

§ 3. No student neglecting or refusing to perform the part assigned him shall receive his degree.

§ 4. No candidate for a degree in any school shall be entitled to receive the same until he shall have discharged all his dues to the college.

CHAPTER IX.

OF VACATIONS.

§ 1. There shall be a vacation of all the schools from the second Wednesday in June until the first Monday in October.

§ 2. There shall be an intermission of the public lectures on Ash Wednesday, on Good Friday, on public holidays established by law, and on such days in each year as may be recommended by the civil authority to be observed as days of fast or thanksgiving; and for two weeks, commencing on the fourth Monday in December, unless the fourth Monday shall fall later than the twenty-sixth day of the month, and in that case commencing with the third Monday.

§ 3. The president may, in extraordinary cases, grant an intermission for other days, not exceeding one day at any one time; and it shall be his duty always to report the same at the next succeeding meeting of the trustees, together with the object and the reason for granting such intermission.

§ 4. No professor or other officer of the college shall excuse a class or section from assembling at the time and place appointed for lecture and recitation, or dismiss a class or section after it may have assembled before the expiration of the time allotted to the exercise, without the consent of the president; nor, without such consent, shall any class or section be excused from the performance of any exercise required of them.

. *PART II.*

THE SCHOOL OF ARTS.

CHAPTER I.

OF THE PRESIDENT.

§ 1. The president shall have power to grant leave of absence for reasonable cause, and for such length of time as he shall judge the occasion may require. Such leave of absence shall be entered upon the minutes of the faculty.

§ 2. He shall assemble the classes every day except Saturday and Sunday, at a convenient hour, to be fixed by the faculty, for the purpose of attending prayers; and at these daily prayers it shall be the duty of each of the members of the faculty to be present, unless his presence shall be dispensed with by the president.

CHAPTER II.

OF THE BOARD OF THE COLLEGE.

§ 1. The faculty of the School of Arts shall consist of the president and the professors engaged in the course of instruction, and shall constitute " The Board of the College." Instructors and tutors shall have seats at the board on all occasions when the conduct or proficiency of the students under their charge, in the departments in which they respectively give instruction, shall be in question, but on no other occasion ; but they shall have no vote.

§ 2. The Board of the College shall appoint a secretary, whose duty it shall be to keep minutes of their proceedings, and to superintend the necessary printing of all the schools, the annual and sextennial registers, and the general handbook. He shall receive a compensation therefor, to be fixed by the trustees.

§ 3. The board shall hold meetings at least once a week during term time.

CHAPTER III.

OF ADMISSION.

§ 1. No student shall be admitted to the freshman class, at its formation, unless he shall have attained the age of fifteen years; nor to a more advanced standing without a corresponding increase of age; but this rule may be dispensed with when, in the opinion of the faculty, there are sufficient reasons to justify its relaxation.

§ 2. Every candidate for admission shall be required to present, before examination, a certificate of good moral character from his last teacher, or from some citizen in good standing; and students from other colleges shall be required to bring certificates from those colleges of honorable discharge.

§ 3. Every applicant for admission shall be examined in such subjects as the faculty may from time to time prescribe. All the requirements for admission shall be annually published.

§ 4. No candidate shall be admitted to an advanced standing until he shall have passed a satisfactory examination upon the studies which have been pursued by the class for which he applies, as well as upon those required for admission.

§ 5. Students desiring to pursue one or more subjects of study less than a full course shall be required to matriculate as special students, and shall be permitted to attend any such course as the faculty may approve, and they may be found qualified to enter upon; but they will not be regarded as candidates for degrees.

CHAPTER IV.

OF THE COURSE OF STUDY.

§ 1. There shall be four classes of undergraduate students in the School of Arts, to be called the freshman class, the sophomore class, the junior class, and the senior class. The course of study of each of these classes shall occupy a year, and the entire course four years.

§ 2. A plan of the course, specifying in detail the studies to be pursued in each year, and in each of the departments of instruction, shall from time to time be prepared by the faculty.

CHAPTER V.

OF DEGREES.

§ 1. Every student in the undergraduate department who shall have completed the entire course of four years, and shall have passed satisfactorily all the examinations required of him, shall be qualified to receive the degree of bachelor of arts, bachelor of letters, or bachelor of science.

PART III.

THE SCHOOL OF MINES.

CHAPTER I.

OF THE FACULTY.

§ 1. The faculty of the School of Mines shall consist of the president and the professors engaged in giving instruction in the school.

§ 2. The faculty shall be authorized to elect a dean from among their own number, who shall be charged with such duties as the president may delegate to him.

§ 3. The faculty shall hold stated meetings at least once a month during term time.

CHAPTER II.

OF ADMISSION.

§ 1. No student shall be admitted to the first class, at its formation, unless he shall have attained the age of eighteen years ; nor to a more advanced standing without a corresponding increase of age ; but this rule may be dispensed with when, in the opinion of the faculty, there are sufficient reasons to justify its relaxation.

§ 2. The requirements for admission shall be prescribed by the faculty of the school, and shall be annually published.

§ 3. No candidate shall be admitted to advanced standing until he shall have passed a satisfactory examination upon the studies which have been pursued by the class for which he applies; but graduates and students of colleges and schools of science in good standing, who shall have completed so much of the course of study as shall be equivalent to the requirements for admission to the school, may be admitted at the beginning of the second year, or earlier, without examination, on presenting diplomas or certificates of good standing and honorable discharge, satisfactory to the examining officers.

CHAPTER III.

OF THE COURSE OF STUDY.

§ 1. There shall be four classes of undergraduate students in the school, to be distinguished as the first, second, third, and fourth classes. The course of study of each of these classes shall occupy a year; and the entire course four years.

§ 2. The subjects of study shall be so grouped as to form seven independent courses of instruction, viz., a course in civil engineering, a course in mining engineering, a course in metallurgy, a course in geology and paleontology, a course in analytical and applied chemistry, a course in architecture, and a course in sanitary engineering. At the beginning of the first year, each student shall elect which of the seven courses above mentioned he intends to pursue, and, after having made his election, he shall not be permitted to abandon the course chosen in order to take up another without the consent of the faculty, to be given only for reasons of weight, to be stated in the minutes.

§ 3. A plan of the several courses, specifying in detail the studies to be pursued in each year, and in each department of instruction, shall from time to time be prepared by the faculty.

CHAPTER IV.

OF DEGREES.

§ 1. Every student who shall have completed the entire course of four years, and shall have passed satisfactorily all the examinations required of him, shall be qualified to receive the degree of engineer of mines, civil engineer, sanitary engineer, metallurgical engineer, or bachelor of philosophy.

PART IV.

THE SCHOOL OF LAW.

CHAPTER I.

OF THE WARDEN.

§ 1. It shall be the duty of the warden to see that the course of instruction prescribed is faithfully pursued, and due discipline observed; to keep himself informed of the manner and efficiency of instruction in the several departments; with the approval of the president to call special meetings of the faculty; and to give such directions and perform such acts as shall, in his judgment, promote the interests of the school, so that they do not contravene the charters, the statutes, the orders of the trustees, or the decisions of the faculty of the school; to give to the president of the college and to the committee on the School of Law, from time to time, any information which he or they may require as to the condition or administration of the school, or as to the manner or efficiency of the instruction, or the performance of duty of any of its officers.

§ 2. He shall have the power, with the approval of the president, to grant leave of absence to individual students, for such length of time as the occasion may require.

§ 3. He shall sign all diplomas for degrees duly conferred.

CHAPTER II.

OF THE FACULTY.

The faculty shall consist of the president of the college, the warden, and the professors of the school. They shall meet statedly once a month during the annual term. In the absence of the president, the warden, or, in the absence of both, the senior professor present, shall preside.

CHAPTER III.

OF ADMISSION.

§ 1. All graduates of literary colleges in good standing, and all persons duly certified to have passed the regents' examination required by the rules of the Court of Appeals of the State of New York, will be admitted without examination. Other candidates for admission must be at least eighteen years of age, and shall be required to pass an examination in such subjects as the faculty may from time to time prescribe. All the requirements for admission shall be annually published.

§ 2. Such examinations shall be conducted by examiners, alumni of the college, to be appointed by the committee on the School of Law.

§ 3. The examinations shall be held during the week next preceding the first Monday in October, and shall be conducted in such form and manner as may be prescribed by the faculty.

CHAPTER IV.

OF THE COURSE OF STUDY.

§ 1. There shall be three classes of undergraduate students in the Law School, to be called respectively the senior, the middle, and the junior class. The course of study of each of these classes shall occupy a year, and the entire course three years.

§ 2. The annual term in the Law School shall commence on the first Monday in October, in each and every year, and shall close on the second Wednesday in June. The annual term shall constitute the collegiate year.

§ 3. A plan of the course, specifying in detail the studies to be pursued in each year, and in each of the departments of instruction, shall from time to time be prepared by the faculty.

§ 4. The warden, with the concurrence of the faculty, shall have power to arrange the hours for lectures and recitations, as well as to select the text-books for the use of the students.

§ 5. Moot courts shall be held under the direction of the faculty, at such times as they may deem proper. The mode of proceeding and the assignments of students to take part in the discussion shall be under the direction of the warden.

CHAPTER V.

OF DEGREES.

§ 1. Every student who shall pass an approved examination upon the required studies of the course shall be entitled to be recommended to the trustees for the degree of bachelor of laws. Should the student not have attained the age of twenty-one years at the time of graduating, the delivery of the diploma shall be deferred until he shall have attained that age.

§ 2. A student who shall not have pursued the full course of study shall be entitled to a certificate, stating the duration of his attendance and the degree of his attainment, to be signed by the warden.

PART V.

THE SCHOOL OF POLITICAL SCIENCE.

CHAPTER I.

OF THE FACULTY.

§ 1. The faculty of the School of Political Science shall consist of the president and the professors engaged in the course of instruction.

§ 2. The faculty shall be authorized to elect a dean from among their own number, who shall be charged with such duties as the president may delegate to him. The term of office of the dean shall be five years. No salary shall be attached to such office.

§ 3. The faculty shall hold stated meetings at least once a month during term time. Instructors in departments not otherwise represented, who are giving permanent instruction, upon the invitation of the faculty may take part in their deliberations, but without a vote.

CHAPTER II.

OF ADMISSION.

Candidates for a degree in this school must have success-fully pursued a course of undergraduate study in this college, or in some other maintaining an equivalent course of study, to the close of the junior year.

CHAPTER III.

OF THE COURSE OF STUDY.

§ 1. There shall be three classes of students in the School of Political Science. The course of study in each of these classes shall occupy a year, and the entire course three years.

§ 2. The course of study shall be designed to prepare young men for the duties of public life, and shall embrace the history of philosophy ; the history of the literature of the political sciences ; the general constitutional history of Europe ; the special constitutional history of England and the United States ; the Roman law and the jurisprudence of existing codes derived therefrom ; the comparative constitutional law of European states and of the United States ; the comparative constitutional law of the different states of the American Union ; the history of diplomacy ; international law ; systems of administration, state and national, of the United States ; comparison of American and European systems of administration ; political economy, and statistics.

§ 3. A plan of the course, specifying in detail the studies to be pursued in each year, shall from time to time be prepared by the faculty.

CHAPTER IV.

OF DEGREES.

Students of the school who shall satisfactorily complete the studies of the first year shall be qualified, on examination and the recommendation of the faculty, to receive the degree of bachelor of philosophy ; or (with the concurrence of the faculty of arts) the degree of bachelor of arts.

PART VI.

THE SCHOOL OF PHILOSOPHY.

CHAPTER I.

OF THE FACULTY.

§ 1. The faculty of the School of Philosophy shall consist of the president and the professors engaged in the course of instruction.

§ 2. The faculty shall be authorized to elect a dean from among their own number, who shall be charged with such duties as the president may delegate to him. But the dean of the faculty of philosophy shall in no case be the same person as the dean of the School of Arts or the secretary of the Board of the College. The term of office of the dean shall be five years. No salary shall be attached to such office.

§ 3. The faculty shall hold stated meetings at least once a month during term time. Instructors in departments not otherwise represented, who are giving permanent instruction, upon the invitation of the faculty may take part in their deliberations, but without a vote.

CHAPTER II.

OF ADMISSION.

Candidates for a degree in this school must have success-fully pursued a course of undergraduate study in this college, or in some other maintaining an equivalent course of study, to the close of the junior year.

CHAPTER III.

OF THE COURSE OF STUDY.

The course of study shall embrace instruction in logic; psychology; ethics; history of philosophy; pædagogics; the Greek language and literature, to include epigraphy and archæology; the Latin language and literature, to include epigraphy and archæology; the English language and lit-erature, to include Anglo-Saxon and Gothic; the Teutonic languages and literatures; the Romance languages and literatures; Sanskrit and Zend; and the Semitic languages.

CHAPTER IV.

OF DEGREES.

Students of the school who shall satisfactorily complete the studies of the first year shall be qualified, on examination and the recommendation of the faculty, to receive the degree of bachelor of philosophy; or (with the concurrence of the faculty of arts) the degree of bachelor of arts.

PART VII.

THE UNIVERSITY COUNCIL.

CHAPTER I.

§ 1. The University Council shall consist of twelve members, as follows:

From the Faculty of Philosophy,	The Dean,	
	One elected member.	2
" " " Political Science,	The Dean,	
	One elected member.	2
" " " Mines,	The Dean,	
	One elected member.	2
" " " Law,	The Warden,	
	One elected member.	2
" " School of Arts, ex-officio,	The Dean,	
	Secretary of the	
	Board of the College.	2
To be selected by the president, with especial reference to securing rounded representation of subjects,		2

§ 2. The president shall make his selections after the elections by the several faculties.

§ 3. The terms of the elected and the selected members of the council shall be three years, and those first chosen shall arrange themselves by lot in classes, so that two shall retire every twelve months.

§ 4. The council shall be called together by the president for consultation, as often as, and whenever, it may seem to him desirable to do so, and with his approval it may provide for stated meetings.

§ 5. The president, if present, shall preside at all meetings of the council, and in case of a meeting in his absence, the meeting shall be presided over by one of their own number elected by the meeting as chairman, *pro-tem.*

§ 6. The whole body of professors represented by delegates in the University Council may be summoned by the president for consultation, as often as, and whenever, it may seem to him desirable to do so.

CHAPTER II.

The University Council shall be an advisory body. In particular it shall advise the president as to all matters affecting the master's and the doctor's degree, the correlation of courses, the extension of university work in new and old fields, and generally as to such matters as the president may bring before it.

PART VIII.

DEGREES.

CHAPTER I.

§ 1. No one shall be eligible for the master's degree who has not obtained his first degree either in arts, in science, in law, in letters, or in philosophy, in Columbia College, or in some other institution maintaining an equivalent curriculum, and who has not followed thereafter, for not less than one year, a course of study satisfactory to the president, under one or more of the university faculties of law, mines, political science, or philosophy. Recommendations for the master's degree may proceed from any one or more of these faculties. The president in all such matters shall advise with the University Council, for the purpose of securing equality of requirement in the different schools.

§ 2. The master's degree may be given for study in absentia, after a three years' course of study approved by the president, to an alumnus of the college in any of its schools, who shall present himself for examination, and shall satisfactorily pass such examination.

CHAPTER II.

No one shall be eligible for the doctor's degree who has not obtained his first degree either in arts, in science, in law, in letters, or in philosophy, in Columbia College, or in some other institution maintaining an equivalent curriculum, and who has not followed thereafter, for not less than two years, a course of study satisfactory to the president, under one or more of the university faculties of law, mines, political science, or philosophy. Recommendations for the doctor's degree may proceed from any one or more of these faculties. The president in all such matters shall advise with the University Council, for the purpose of securing equality of requirement in the different schools.

CHAPTER III.

§ 1. All work hitherto known as graduate work shall hereafter be called university work, and in all matters affecting such work the faculties having it in charge shall vote by departments. All graduate work hitherto carried on in connection with the School of Arts, in subjects covered by the faculty of philosophy, shall hereafter be under the charge of the faculty of philosophy. All graduate work in mathematics and the natural and applied sciences, whether now carried on in connection with the School of Arts or the School of Mines, shall hereafter be under the charge of the faculty of the School of Mines.

§ 2. The faculties having charge of university work shall have power to formulate the courses they propose to offer. Suggestions as to combinations of courses and the like, emanating from the council, shall go into effect only upon the approval of all the faculties concerned. Either the council or any faculty may submit questions for consideration to each other.

PART IX.

OF AMENDMENTS.

No amendment, alteration, or repeal of these statutes, or of any part thereof, shall be made until four weeks after the same shall have been presented in writing at a meeting of the trustees.

www.ingramcontent.com/pod-product-compliance
Lightning Source LLC
Chambersburg PA
CBHW021609270326
41931CB00009B/1405